The *7* Rings of MARRIAGE™

Practical Biblical Wisdom
for Every Season of Your Marriage

JACKIE BLEDSOE

LifeWay Press®
Nashville, Tennessee

ISBN 9781430042754 Item 005753519

Dewey decimal classification: 306.81 • Subject headings: MARRIAGE / DOMESTIC RELATIONS / MARRIED PEOPLE

Unless otherwise noted, Scripture quotations are from Holman Christian Standard Bible®, Copyright ©1999, 2000, 2002, 2003, 2009 by Holman Bible Publishers. Used by permission. Holman Christian Standard Bible® and HCSB® are federally registered trademarks of Holman Bible Publishers. Scripture taken from the Holy Bible, NEW INTERNATIONAL VERSION®. Copyright © 1973, 1978, 1984, 2011 by Biblica, Inc. All rights reserved worldwide. Used by permission.

To order additional copies of this resource, write to LifeWay Church Resources Customer Service; One LifeWay Plaza; Nashville, TN 37234-0113; fax 615.251.5933; phone toll free 800.458.2772; email *orderentry@lifeway.com*, order online at *www.lifeway.com*, or visit the LifeWay Christian Store serving you.

Printed in the United States of America

Adult Ministry Publishing, LifeWay Church Resources, One LifeWay Plaza, Nashville, TN 37234-0152

CONTENTS

ABOUT THE AUTHOR

Jackie Bledsoe is a professional blogger, author, and speaker, but first and foremost a husband and father who encourages men to better lead and love their families. He's a contributor to *All Pro Dad*, Disney's *Babble.com*, *The Good Men Project*, and *Huffington Post*. His work has also been featured on *Yahoo!*, *USA Football*, *MichaelHyatt.com*, *Black and Married with Kids*, *Coach Up*, and more.

Jackie and his wife, Stephana, have been friends since they were teenagers, more than half of their lives, and will celebrate 15 years of marriage in June 2016. They are the proud parents of three beautiful children, and together they co-host *The 7 Rings of Marriage™ Show*, where they share practical marriage lessons and interview couples who have lasting and fulfilling marriages.

The Bledsoes reside in Indianapolis and have a heart for marriage forged through God's grace in their own marriage, which has thrived through homelessness (twice!), job loss and financial despair, loneliness, and in-law and intimacy issues. Their desire is for God to use their story as one of hope and inspiration to other marriages.

Find more about Jackie on his blog, *JackieBledsoe.com*, where he offers some amazing resources created to help you have a lasting and fulfilling marriage and meaningful influence on your kids.

You can also get additional free *7 Rings of Marriage Bible Study* resources at *www.jackiebledsoe.com/7RingsResources*.

Want to connect with Jackie? Visit his website, *JackieBledsoe.com*, and find out how to book him for your next event, read his blog, and connect with him on Facebook, Instagram, and Twitter. Jackie loves meeting and connecting with new people, so be sure to stop by and say hello!

HOW TO USE THIS STUDY

Welcome to *The 7 Rings of Marriage* Bible study created to give you practical biblical wisdom for every season of your marriage. I hope your group experiences results as they gain a greater understanding of God's design for a lasting and fulfilling marriage and the important role your marriage serves for your family, friends, community, and—ultimately—the body of Christ.

The 7 Rings of Marriage Bible study is an 8-session study. Most groups meet weekly, completing one session per week, but feel free to follow a plan that meets the needs and schedule of the couples in your group.

To make the best use of this study, your first session together will be your introduction. Use this session as a way to break the ice, have some fun, get to know each other better, and prepare to venture together through each of the 7 Rings.

Be sure each couple receives a copy of the Bible study book during the first session so they come prepared for following group meetings.

Each session consists of two major sections of content, each with its own features, purpose, and means of interaction: group time and couple time.

GROUP TIME

START. This section includes questions the group leaders can use to get the conversation started and introduce the video segment of the session. Some questions will ask you to reflect back on your activity from a previous section. Other questions can be used as icebreakers to jumpstart discussions.

WATCH. Stephana and I will lead a teaching time on the topic for each session. Watching the video together and taking notes will enrich your discussion and provide additional insight into the session's discussion questions.

DISCUSS. This section includes questions, statements, and passages of Scripture that build on the lessons taught in the video. Each couple will be able to participate and benefit from the discussion just by showing up for each session. Small groups have been an important part of our marriage, and we believe they will be for your marriage too.

We suggest briefly working through the questions as couples before discussing them with the group, allowing you to better prepare yourself to share what God has revealed through the videos. If you get stuck, ask for the insight of other couples in the group during the discussion time.

WRAP-UP. After ending your group discussion you will find some key points listed that will serve as highlights from your time together. Use these points to re-emphasize the primary message of each session.

PRAY. As a group, spend time in prayer. Pray *for* and *with* each other as you go through this journey of understanding and growing in your marriages. Use the points to help guide your prayers.

COUPLE TIME

MARRIAGE ENRICHMENT ACTIVITIES. In each session I've provided some practical steps to help you put into action what you've learned from God's Word about marriage. Spend the first few days after your group session to do these activities.

Feel free to refer to your group discussion notes, key points, and Scriptures as a refresher in completing the activities. We suggest scheduling the time to do these activities in your calendars.

DATE NIGHT. I included a few date night ideas at the end of each session. Enjoy time with your spouse each week by completing one of the dates or choose a date night idea of your own. Note that at least one of the date night ideas included will be directly related to the key points in the current session. Date night is an important part of the study—and your marriage overall—and you don't want to miss out on it.

Let's get started!

Go to *jackiebledsoe.com/7RingsResources* for a free marriage devotional and more marriage resources.

HOW TO USE THIS STUDY   7

SESSION 1:
BEGIN WITH THE END

"Will you take _____ to be your lawfully wedded..."

If you're reading this, then you have answered—or perhaps are soon to be answering—that question. Hopefully, you've made the choice to live out the promise that follows as best as you can: *"for better or for worse."*

The good news is the "better" can be way better than the worse. While none of our marriages are perfect, there is a perfect plan and purpose for them. In the Book of Genesis, we see how God created this institution of marriage to meet some of our deepest desires and needs but also to play a part in His magnificent plan for humanity.

God's design was that we would reach a level of intimacy in marriage that isn't possible through any other relationship with any other human being. He wants that for us. He wants that for you.

And when intimacy happens, not only are our own desires met, but His purpose is fulfilled and He is glorified. So, let's begin this journey together with the help, support, and accountability of those who've chosen to journey with us. And let's experience marriages that are both lasting and fulfilling.

Welcome to the first group session.

If this is your first time meeting as a group, or if there are new couples, take a few minutes for couples to introduce themselves. Ask everyone to share their names, how long they've been married/engaged, and if/how many children they have.

WATCH

GOAL: To understand why we get married and define the purpose of marriage.

WATCH SESSION 1: "BEGIN WITH THE END." Use the following statements to follow along and record key quotes and ideas that stand out to you on the notes page.

Marriage is risky when we look for fulfillment in the wrong places.

There is a greater purpose for my marriage than my happiness.

God has given us a guide for marriage and with it comes hope.

Marriage is not just for you, it's for your spouse and everyone else connected to you.

Our start doesn't have to determine our finish.

A lasting and fulfilling marriage will require a significant investment on your part.

You have to be willing to take a hard stance in your marriage.

DISCUSS

God laid out a miraculous plan and purpose for marriage in the Book of Genesis beginning with the creation of the world and the story of the first husband and wife.

This first union between Adam and Eve and the commands God gave them apply to our marriages this very day. These commands are not outdated but are as relevant now as they were when God instituted the first marriage.

Let's see exactly what God did and said to Adam and Eve and then discuss how that relates to our own marriages.

READ GENESIS 2:18-25 AND THEN DISCUSS THE FOLLOWING QUESTIONS.
(You may want to discuss questions first as couples or in small groups of two or four for a few minutes and then share your answers with the larger group.)

What does this passage say Adam was missing, or lacking?

In what ways do you and your spouse complement each other?

What were the barriers, if any, between Adam and Eve?

What prevents you from being truly vulnerable with your spouse?

God's intention for marriage from the beginning was for man and woman to come together as one (v. 24) and find fulfillment in each other.

READ GENESIS 1:26-31 AND PROVERBS 5:18.

What blessing did God give man (and woman)?

How has God blessed your marriage as you think about how you and your spouse are created in God's image?

What did God command Adam and Eve to do?

In what ways can you steward your marriage so that your spouse, family, friends, and community benefit?

READ HEBREWS 13:4A.

What does this verse say about how we should view or hold marriage?

Share examples of how you have seen this done? How have you seen marriage disrespected?

WRAP-UP

Your marriage has a God-given purpose.

God created Eve to be Adam's perfect complement and helper. One of the primary roles in your marriage, whether husband or wife, is to serve your spouse.

Your marriage can be fruitful and fulfilling, no matter the circumstances, but you have to know its purpose and keep your eyes set on what God can accomplish.

PRAY

Spend the next few minutes praying with and for one another. Use the points below for guidance.

Thank God for your spouse and the amazing things He can do through your marriage.

Pray that God will open your eyes to see your spouse as He does. Ask God to help you focus more on your spouse than yourself.

Ask God to give you wisdom as you seek His instruction and apply it to your life and marriage.

MARRIAGE ENRICHMENT ACTIVITIES

ACTIVITY 1

Answer the following questions as a couple on your own. Respond according to your season of life or marriage.

READ PROVERBS 18:22.

> *A man who finds a wife finds a good thing*
> *and obtains favor from the Lord.*

Do you consider your marriage to be a "good thing" from the Lord? Why or why not?

How has our culture hindered many people from seeing marriage as a gift?

Think back to the Engagement RING period in your relationship. What were the top reasons you wanted to marry your spouse?

What thoughts and feelings did you experience?

When we say "I do" we have many different thoughts, feelings, and emotions. After a while, we learn that these "feelings" can sometimes come and go. Reflecting on the moments when these emotions and feelings were strongest is a fun exercise, but it's also a great reminder of why you married one other.

As you move through each of the 7 Rings, it's good to remember where it all started.

Before the next group session plan a time to watch your wedding videos, look at wedding and engagement photos, or talk about that special day when you said "I do."

Use the space below and document this experience.

Now that you've reflected on the past, specifically your wedding day, let's begin to look ahead. Goal setting is a great practice that helps successful people become successful. It's also a great practice that helps successful marriages become successful. The "goal" of goal setting is to allow you to imagine or paint a picture of the end result you are looking for—in this case, for your marriage.

READ PHILIPPIANS 2:1-2.

> *If then there is any encouragement in Christ, if any consolation of love, if any fellowship with the Spirit, if any affection and mercy, fulfill my joy by thinking the same way, having the same love, sharing the same feelings, focusing on one goal.*

The "one goal" Paul wanted the Philippians to focus on was their work for the gospel. Are you and your spouse focused on the same goals in your marriage? Explain.

Do you think the same way about what you want your marriage to look like? Do you share the same thoughts and feelings about what a lasting and fulfilling marriage should be? Why or why not?

Spend 15-30 minutes listing goals you have as a married couple. Here are some examples:

I want to renew our wedding vows on our 25th anniversary.

I want to have a marriage that lasts and fulfills everything we both need in marriage.

I want to be the person God uses to help my wife (or husband) discover and fulfill her (or his) dreams and greatest passions.

Now take time to create your own list in the space below and then spend time praying as a couple that God will help you achieve these goals together. Write down any action steps you might take to make these goals a reality.

ACTIVITY 3

READ ROMANS 8:26.

In the same way the Spirit also joins to help in our weakness, because we do not know what to pray for as we should, but the Spirit Himself intercedes for us with unspoken groanings.

Marriage is challenging, and help is always needed. Fortunately, we constantly have help for our marriages, and this help through the Holy Spirit is accessible through prayer. Establishing a habit of prayer is foundational for your marriage relationship to stand through all circumstances

READ EPHESIANS 6:18.

Pray at all times in the Spirit with every prayer and request, and stay alert in this with all perseverance and intercession for all the saints.

What do you think Paul means to "pray at all times"?

What does this look like practically in your marriage?

If you haven't already, establish at least five minutes per day to pray together as a couple. Once you determine the most feasible time when you can accomplish this daily, then schedule it on both of your calendars. Make it non-negotiable. If something unavoidable does come up and you miss that time, be sure to make it up some time the same day. And then get back on track the next day.

Use the space below to record specific prayer requests you have for your marriage. What is the time and place where you will pray together?

DATE NIGHT

Date nights are important, and should be a staple in your marriage. They are also fun and a great way to deepen your connection with your spouse. Choose one (or both) of the following date night ideas to do before the next group session.

OPTION 1—SUNSET/SUNRISE DATE

Choose night (or early morning) to sit together and watch the sunset or sunrise. Prior to doing so, create a playlist of some of your favorite music in iTunes, Spotify, or on a CD. Be sure there are songs you both enjoy.

On your date night (or early morning), grab some chairs, go outside, turn on your music, and enjoy the sunset/sunrise and each other. Here is a conversation starter if needed:

CONVERSATION STARTER: What would you say is your biggest strength? Weakness? How do these strengths and weaknesses bring balance to the marriage relationship?

OPTION 2—SCRAPBOOK DATE

Grab some old photos and special items, some scrapbooking supplies, and your favorite playlist. Spend an evening talking about some of the most memorable experiences you've had as a married couple, and create scrapbook pages to fill your book.

CONVERSATION STARTER: What are some of the best times we've had as a couple?

SESSION 2:
ENGAGEMENT *RING*

"Will you marry me?"

These four words are some of the most life-changing words ever said or heard. When the word "yes" follows, these two people's lives will never be the same, but the actions taken between "yes" and "I do" will help determine the long-term outcome of that change. During this time, building a strong foundation will lead to a strong marriage.

A season filled with hope, love, and possibility, it can be easy to neglect some important building blocks during this engagement season. Even if you are well past the engagement stage of your marriage, you may still be guilty of neglecting these building blocks. Foundation building is vital at the beginning and throughout our marriages.

Welcome to the second group session.

Session 1 focused on God's purpose of marriage and how we see our marriages in relation to this purpose.

> What was most helpful, encouraging, or challenging from your couple time activities from the previous session?

In this session, we'll begin to focus on building a strong foundation to create a strong marriage.

WATCH

GOAL: To build our marriages on the Rock.

WATCH SESSION 2: "ENGAGEMENT RING." Use the following statements to follow along and record key quotes and ideas that stand out to you on the notes page.

The good stuff happens when we get beneath the surface.

The foundation might not seem as important at first, but it is vital.

Success comes from a relational, not transactional focus.

You must set your marriage in reference to the Cornerstone.

Strengthening your foundation makes it last.

You need the right mixture for your foundation.

DISCUSS

Most metropolitan downtown areas have huge buildings—much bigger than the houses and structures you find in residential neighborhoods. Because of the soaring height of the downtown buildings, they must have stronger and deeper foundations than our houses. There's no way the skyscraper could stand on the same foundation that supports a home.

Our marriages work in similar ways. The strongest and deepest foundations create the longest lasting and most fulfilling marriages. The weakest and most shallow foundations create the shortest and most frustrating marriages.

Much like the engineers who create the plans and set the course for structural foundations, God has done the same thing for your marriage. His blueprint shows you where to start, how to get beneath the surface, and how to strengthen your marriage foundation.

READ MATTHEW 7:24-29 AND THEN DISCUSS THE FOLLOWING QUESTIONS.

Based on what we learned from Matthew 7:24-29, what does building your house on a "rock" mean?

The wise and foolish men in Matthew 7 were both exposed to the same storms. And both heard the same words. With that being the case, what's the primary difference between the wise man and the foolish man?

How does your marriage compare? How do your actions, or inactions, reflect obedience or disobedience to God's Word?

What practical steps can you take to keep your marriage house on the Rock?

WRAP-UP

Our marriages are best when they are set on the Rock—on our faith in Christ. The actions in our marriage must be carefully and consistently measured against the principles of the Bible—God's blueprint for our lives and marriages.

PRAY

Spend the next few minutes praying with and for one another. Use the points below for guidance.

Thank God for the good thing He's given us with marriage.

If you haven't already, ask God to help you make Him the center of your marriage.

Ask God to help you carve out time each day for prayer and for Bible study to guide you as you seek to obey His Word.

MARRIAGE ENRICHMENT ACTIVITIES

We best find solutions to our problems, answers to our questions, and direction for our marriages through regular communication with God through prayer and Bible study. In this activity we will focus on prayer.

READ PHILIPPIANS 4:6-7 THEN ANSWER THE FOLLOWING QUESTIONS.

Don't worry about anything, but in everything, through prayer and petition with thanksgiving, let your requests be made known to God. And the peace of God, which surpasses every thought, will guard your hearts and minds in Christ Jesus.

How is your individual prayer life? How would you rate it on a scale of 1-6 (6 being "I feel really good about it") and why?

1	2	3	4	5	6

What challenges do you face that prevent you from praying together?

How do you track and celebrate when God answers prayers in your marriage?

In the Bible, God's people were continually encouraged to write down what God had done for them. Without this written record, they may forget what He had done, which they still did many times. A record of God's faithfulness helped His people to remember better and reflect on God's intervention in their lives.

Spend a few minutes together writing down some of your answered prayers and ways God has blessed your marriage. Then write down the prayers you have for your marriage and family today. When God answers those prayers, come back and write what happened next to or under the prayer request.

Be sure to wrap up this activity by taking time to pray together as a couple.

ACTIVITY 2

As we discussed in the group session, building our marriages on the Rock is crucial. The wisdom comes when we act on this knowledge. One of the greatest disciplines we can practice is that of regular prayer—both alone and with our spouses.

One of the activities from Session 1 was to pray at least five minutes per day as a couple. Hopefully you've done that and will continue.

Now it's time to add Bible reading and study. The activity days in between group sessions in this Bible study are a great place to start.

To help you get started this week, let's take a look at why Bible study is important.

READ 2 TIMOTHY 3:16-17.

> *All Scripture is inspired by God and is profitable for teaching, for rebuking, for correcting, for training in righteousness, so that the man of God may be complete, equipped for every good work.*

What is the purpose of Scripture?

Would you consider your marriage a "good work" as mentioned in 2 Timothy 3:17?

God has given us His Word to teach us, to redirect us, and to train us to be more like Him. What are some great ways to consistently read and study the Word together, both alone and as a couple?

Go to *jackiebledsoe.com/7RingsResources* for a free marriage devotional and more marriage resources.

Make time to work through the activity sections and discuss them with your spouse each day. Group sessions are important, but the marriage enrichment activities during the week are absolutely crucial to the success of this study.

What plan do you have in place to read and study the Bible together?

Study 2 Timothy 3 (or another passage) together and use the space below and document your experience studying God's Word.

In your group session this week, we looked at the storms that came against the wise and foolish men in Matthew 7. We must realize those storms can come from various places, even from our spouses. The storm's "actions" were never addressed, only the actions or the response of the person God was speaking to.

READ JAMES 5:16 AND ANSWER THE QUESTIONS BELOW.

> *Therefore, confess your sins to one another and pray for one another, so that you may be healed. The urgent request of a righteous person is very powerful in its effect.*

> What practical actions does this verse suggest that might help us when facing storms in our marriage?

> When you face storms in life do you look inward or outward at the people and circumstances around the storm?

Pray for God to help you look to Him first, and then internally, before you look at external circumstances or people as the source or solution to your problems.

When we are in the midst of hard times, it's good to have Scripture hidden in our hearts that we can quickly refer to for help. It's also good to have a simple principle or guide that we can refer to in decision-making, problem-solving, and those fork-in-the-road moments in our lives and marriages.

This week as you're praying and reading, search for a verse or two that you can refer to for guidance in your marriage. Find your marriage's foundational verse. You can refer back to the verses we've studied or use another verse that is significant to you.

> Write your foundational verse below as well as on a notecard or in your phone. Begin to commit it to memory. You want to have this verse accessible at all times, especially in the storms of life that impact your marriage.

DATE NIGHT

Date nights are important and should be a staple in your marriage. They are also fun and a great way to deepen your connection with your spouse. Choose one (or both) of the following date night ideas to do before the next group session.

OPTION 1—POTTERY DATE

Find a local art or pottery class in your area—something where you can build or create something together. It can even be a painting class. Attend the class, create, and see what you can build together. Here is a conversation starter if needed:

CONVERSATION STARTER: Like a creative design or work of art, marriage is messy and flawed. How would you compare and describe a perfect marriage like a piece of art?

OPTION 2—MOVIE NIGHT AT HOME

Rent a movie, pop some popcorn, grab your favorite sweet snack and beverage, and then enjoy a movie night together at home. We suggest watching a movie like *Courageous* (2011) or *War Room* (2015) that reflect godly values and principles. Here is a conversation starter if needed:

CONVERSATION STARTER: We live in the real world, not a movie. How can I best pray for you?

SESSION 3:
WEDDING *RING*

"With this ring I thee wed. Wear it as a symbol of your love and commitment."

Those of us who are already married said these words, or a variation of them, on our wedding day. If you are engaged, you'll say them one day soon. At this particular moment, it all becomes so real. You are officially married and officially committed. And what a commitment that is!

The Wedding RING is an amazing stage in our marriages. It's a time for shared vision and coming together in all aspects of our lives. New love feels good. Experiencing life as one for the first time feels good. This commitment, this becoming one, is definitely cause for celebration on your wedding day and throughout your marriage.

START

Welcome to the third group session.

Session 2 focused on setting our marriages on the foundation of a relationship with Jesus Christ so that our marriages stand tall and strong!

> What was most helpful, encouraging, or challenging from your couple time activities from the previous session?

In this session we'll begin to focus on our commitment in marriage, coming together as one, and remaining together as one.

WATCH

GOAL: To commit to being one in all areas of our marriage.

WATCH SESSION 3: "WEDDING RING." Use the statements below to follow along and record key quotes and ideas that stand out to you on the notes page.

> We must not allow anything to prevent us from coming together as one.

> We have to be fully committed, not partially or conditionally.

> Divorce is not an option.

> If we are to truly become one, having a shared vision is vital.

> When you fail to plan in marriage, you plan to fail in marriage.

> Getting help, or counseling, is a wise choice, not a desperate one.

DISCUSS

In marriage, we are called to commit to our spouses in a way that is unlike any other relationship we have. A partial commitment won't do. A commitment based on our spouse's actions won't do.

God calls us to fully commit.

READ GENESIS 2:19-24 AND MATTHEW 19:4-6 AND THEN DISCUSS THE FOLLOWING QUESTIONS.

> Matthew 19:5 quotes Genesis 2:24, saying a man is to leave his father and mother and become one with his wife. Why is this so important?

While sexual intercourse may be one of the first things that pops into your mind when you think of coming together as one—and rightfully so, as sex is one of the greatest tools for intimacy that God gives us—there is more.

> What are some other practical ways you can become one in your marriage?

READ MALACHI 2:13-16 AND THEN DISCUSS THE FOLLOWING QUESTIONS AND STATEMENTS.

Verse 16 uses the words "hates" and "divorces" together, followed by "he covers his garment with injustice" (HCSB) or "does violence to the one he should protect" (NIV). God views divorce as a hateful and violent act. It goes against the commitment vow made during the wedding ceremony and against God's design for a lasting marriage covenant.

> According to this passage, why does God view divorce as such a treacherous act?

> How does this affect your perception of divorce and how God views your commitment to your spouse?

(Note: While God takes divorce seriously, it is not an act that is beyond His grace and forgiveness. For anyone doing this study who has already experienced the heartbreak of divorce, talk to your leader about resources available to you that can help as you move forward.)

We are made in God's image, and marriage is designed to be an example of a covenant relationship to the world.

READ PROVERBS 11:14.

Whether your marriage is on the brink of divorce or you are seeing some of your best days so far, wise counsel is good for all seasons of our marriage. What are some practical ways you can receive wise counsel throughout your marriage?

WRAP-UP

Becoming one with your spouse is God's plan for marriage. We should not allow anything to come between us and our spouses. Getting help is not bad, it is actually one of the wisest things we can do.

PRAY

Spend the next few minutes praying with and for one another. Use the points below for guidance.

Thank God for creating many ways for you to express coming together as one.

Pray against anything you've allowed to come between you and your covenant relationship with your spouse and anything that could potentially do so.

Ask God to guide you in planning for a marriage that lasts.

Pray that God sends wise counselors and peers to help you in your marriage.

MARRIAGE ENRICHMENT ACTIVITIES

READ LUKE 14:28-30.

> *For which of you, wanting to build a tower, doesn't first sit down*
> *and calculate the cost to see if he has enough to complete it?*
> *Otherwise, after he has laid the foundation and cannot finish*
> *it, all the onlookers will begin to make fun of him, saying,*
> *"This man started to build and wasn't able to finish."*

In the group session this week, we discussed how God views divorce. Considering how God sees divorce and the impact it has on all relationships, even our relationship with God, we must take the marriage commitment seriously. A wedding ceremony is normally a lavish, extravagant celebration, of which the occasion is worthy. But failure will come when a couple only plans for the wedding and not the life together in marriage after the wedding ceremony.

While this passage in Luke is teaching on the cost of following Christ, we can apply the same principles to our marriages.

What will it actually take to have the marriage you were hoping for on your wedding day?

How can you make plans today to work toward a marriage that is lasting, fulfilling, and glorifying to God?

READ MATTHEW 19:6.

*So they are no longer two, but one flesh. Therefore, what
God has joined together, man must not separate.*

Through the years, we've used various symbols to signify the joining together of two
people in marriage. Sometimes at weddings we see unity candles, braided twine or rope,
or other items mixed together that cannot be separated.

Use the space below and list other examples that illustrate the unity
of marriage and then spend time praying over your commitment to
each other.

REREAD MALACHI 2:14-15 THAT YOU STUDIED IN YOUR GROUP SESSION THIS WEEK.

Yet you ask, "For what reason?" Because the Lord has been a witness between you and the wife of your youth. You have acted treacherously against her, though she was your marriage partner and your wife by covenant. Didn't the one God make us with a remnant of His life-breath? And what does the One seek? A godly offspring. So watch yourselves carefully, and do not act treacherously against the wife of your youth.

In verse 14 the words *marriage partner* are used to illustrate the bond we have in marriage. This description of our marriage means that, like a partnership, we have common goals in addition to the commitment to each other. We have a joint interest in seeing this partnership succeed.

Do you have written goals for your life together? If so, share and discuss one of your marriage goals with your spouse.

Share some great ideas for marriage goals that you would like to establish.

Throughout the week begin to think and pray about the goals you'd like to accomplish in your life. Before the next session, share them with one another. Together, create at least one shared goal and then determine how you can work together to help each spouse achieve his or her respective "individual" goals.

Use the space below to record both your individual and shared goals, and then spend time praying for each other and your goals. What action steps will you take to help your spouse accomplish those goals?

ACTIVITY 3

In Session 2, we discussed laying the foundation of your marriage on the Rock—Jesus Christ. In this week's group session, we discussed the importance of planning for a successful marriage.

Remember, if you fail to plan in marriage, you plan to fail in marriage.

READ PROVERBS 24:27 AND ANSWER THE QUESTION BELOW.

Complete your outdoor work, and prepare your field; afterward, build your house.

If you've laid your marriage foundation correctly, what are you building your house on?

READ PROVERBS 15:22 AND ANSWER THE QUESTIONS BELOW.

Plans fail when there is no counsel, but with many advisers they succeed.

What is the key to successfully fulfilling your plans in marriage?

What are your initial thoughts when it comes to receiving advice, mentoring, accountability, or counseling in marriage? Why?

Have you ever considered counseling, mentoring, and accountability as a way to prevent potential marriage storms? Why or why not?

From premarriage to the wedding day, and from the wedding day and beyond, receiving counsel can help your marriage succeed. It is important to allow others to speak truth into your life and marriage. Wise counsel, mentoring, and accountability are not only needed during desperate times, they are needed during good times as well.

Reach out to some couples you trust, who may or may not be part of this group, and ask them who they turn to for marriage advice. Write down the names of these trusted advisors and begin praying together for God to guide you to someone to help your marriage when needed. Make this a part of your marriage success plan.

Date Night

Date nights are important and should be a staple in your marriage. They are also fun and a great way to deepen your connection with your spouse. Choose one (or both) of the following date night ideas to do before the next group session.

OPTION 1—PREPARE AND ENJOY A HOME-COOKED MEAL

Plan to prepare a home-cooked meal together. Start by deciding on a meal, shopping for the ingredients, and then get in the kitchen to prep, cook, and enjoy the meal together.

CONVERSATION STARTER: What can we do as a couple to make a change in our community?

OPTION 2—GOLF OR TENNIS "DOUBLES DATE"

Challenge another couple to a round of golf or a match of tennis (or even putt-putt)—you and your spouse against the other couple. If you can't or don't play golf or tennis, find another competition you can have where you and your spouse are on a team working together.

CONVERSATION STARTER: One thing I really enjoy doing with you is _____. What is one thing you really enjoy doing with me?

SESSION 4:
DISCOVERING

"I vow to take time to share with you, to listen, and to care ..."

Most of us have completed at least twelve years of school and received a diploma. Some went on to study in college and received an undergraduate degree. A handful kept going and received a master's degree. And a few went even further and received a doctorate degree.

After completing the highest level of our "formal education," we soon discover learning new lessons never stops. Our relationships with our spouses are the same way. After a premarital class, after the wedding, after kids, and even after going through this book, we still need to study—our spouses.

The DiscoveRING is a thread that runs through each ring, helping to bind the rings—and your marriage—together.

START

Welcome to the fourth group session. Session 3 focused on becoming one in marriage and living out our lives this way.

> What was most helpful, encouraging, or challenging from your couple time activities from the previous session?

In this session we'll begin to focus on getting to know our spouse better as we become lifelong learners of each other. In addition we'll focus on the importance of appreciating and embracing our differences.

WATCH

GOAL: To discover new things about your spouse through study and become a lifelong learner of him or her.

WATCH SESSION 4: "DISCOVERING." Use the statements below to follow along, and record key quotes and ideas that stand out to you on the notes page.

> Knowing our spouses involves first knowing who they are in Christ.

> Effective communication is a major key in the discovering of our spouses.

> Differences are fine and when embraced can bless your marriage.

> Change is constant yet our past can impact our present and future.

> You may not marry your best friend but you can eventually be married to your best friend.

> Discovering new things about each other doesn't happen by accident.

> If dating led to marriage then dating can help keep you married.

DISCUSS

Intimacy in our marriages is something we all desire, but it can be interpreted differently depending upon who you ask. A simple way to look at intimacy is that it involves sharing experiences with a person you don't share or experience with anybody else.

In marriage, there is a connection, a oneness that you can't—and shouldn't—get from your friends, your kids, your extended family, your co-workers, or anybody else. We should know our spouses like no one else knows them and vice versa. Some of this comes naturally, but the really deep connection takes more work.

Communication and attentiveness to our spouses is key, but we must also be intentional. God wants us to connect to our spouses. He wants our love and marriage relationship to have more depth than any other relationship we have, except with Him.

Let's take a look at some of the passages that demonstrate this idea and discuss how each applies to our marriages.

READ 1 PETER 3:1-7 AND THEN DISCUSS THE FOLLOWING QUESTIONS.

How is a wife to live with her husband?

When a wife conducts herself in this way, what is the result? Wives, in what practical ways can you do this?

How is a husband to live with his wife and what place is she to have in his life?

What is the result when this happens? Husbands, in what practical ways can you be sensitive to your wife's deepest physical and emotional needs?

READ THE FOLLOWING PASSAGES OF SCRIPTURE: JAMES 1:19, PROVERBS 18:13, AND PROVERBS 18:2.

James 1:19 teaches us an effective formula for communication. What are you quick to do and slow to do in your communication with your spouse?

What is one practical way to avoid foolishness and disgrace in your communication?

How does effective communication relate to better understanding and knowing your spouse?

WRAP-UP

We must know our spouses—who they are in Christ and who they are in relationship to us.

Effective communication can be a bridge or a barrier to better knowing our spouses.

The practice of studying our spouses and our marriages must be a priority.

PRAY

Spend the next few minutes praying with and for one another. Use the points below for guidance.

Thank God for giving you the opportunity to know your spouse in very intimate ways.

Pray that your marriages will be filled with understanding.

Ask God to help you view your spouse as He sees him or her.

Pray for a marriage that has regular and effective communication that is revealing and encouraging for both husband and wife.

MARRIAGE ENRICHMENT ACTIVITIES

ACTIVITY 1

In the Book of Ruth we learn about the story of Ruth and Boaz. Ruth was the daughter-in-law of Naomi. While they were living in the land of Moab, both Naomi's and Ruth's husbands died. Ruth chose to continue living with Naomi and returned with her to Judah to find food—where she met Boaz.

An intriguing part of the story is how Boaz and Ruth learned of each other's family backgrounds. This discovering process would impact their relationship and how intimate they could and would later become.

Read Ruth 2:5-11 and list below everything Boaz discovered about Ruth and her family background from his servants.

READ RUTH 2:19-20.

Then her mother-in-law said to her, "Where did you gather barley today, and where did you work? May the Lord bless the man who noticed you." Ruth told her mother-in-law about the men she had worked with and said, "The name of the man I worked with today is Boaz." Then Naomi said to her daughter-in-law, "May he be blessed by the Lord, who has not forsaken his kindness to the living or the dead." Naomi continued, "The man is a close relative. He is one of our family redeemers."

What does Ruth discover about Boaz from her conversation with Naomi? Do some research about what it meant to have a kinsman-redeemer.

How did these discoveries impact Ruth and Boaz's future relationship?

Learning about your spouse's family background is important as it directly impacts how you relate to each other. Spend time this week discussing your family backgrounds. Discuss what you have learned, who you learned it from, and what impact it has had on your life and marriage.

Use the space below and document this experience, and then pray as a couple that you would both be committed to the discovery process and to learning more about each other.

_____

_____

_____

_____

_____

_____

_____

_____

_____

_____

_____

_____

_____

_____

_____

_____

_____

READ EPHESIANS 4:15 AND 1 CORINTHIANS 13:1, 4-7.

EPHESIANS 4:15
*But speaking the truth in love, let us grow in every
way into Him who is the head—Christ.*

1 CORINTHIANS 13:1, 4-7
*If I speak human or angelic languages but do not have love, I
am a sounding gong or a clanging cymbal. ... Love is patient,
love is kind. Love does not envy, is not boastful, is not conceited,
does not act improperly, is not selfish, is not provoked,
and does not keep a record of wrongs. Love finds no joy in
unrighteousness but rejoices in the truth. It bears all things,
believes all things, hopes all things, endures all things.*

Based on these verses, how should you speak to your spouse?

What happens when your words lack love?

Based on 1 Corinthians 13:4-7, how do you speak to your spouse in love?

This week, have a "truth in love conversation" by asking your spouse to share one thing that has happened recently between you both that hurt or concerned him or her. (Be careful about digging up the past and things that are already resolved.) Then ask your spouse to share what he or she would like to see happen or change, and what he or she is willing to do to make that happen. Listen with the intent to understand completely before you say a word. (Remember James 1:19 from our group session this week?) Once you are satisfied with the outcome of that conversation, it's your turn to share and your spouse's turn to listen.

Remember that no couple has a perfect relationship and marriage. However, by discussing your challenges, hurts, and concerns you keep communication open and your marriage in discoveRING.

> Use the space below and document this experience. Once you are finished, don't forget to pray for each other. Use 1 Corinthians 13:4-7 as a guide and pray that you might be able to exhibit these characteristics of love to your spouse this week.

We should learn to encourage our spouses in all areas, and our words are one of the best ways to do this.

READ THE FOLLOWING PASSAGES AND CONSIDER HOW EACH APPLIES TO YOUR MARRIAGE:

1 THESSALONIANS 5:11
*Therefore encourage one another and build
each other up as you are already doing.*

EPHESIANS 4:29
*No foul language is to come from your mouth, but only what is good for
building up someone in need, so that it gives grace to those who hear.*

PROVERBS 29:11
A fool gives full vent to his anger, but a wise man holds it in check.

PROVERBS 12:18
*There is one who speaks rashly, like a piercing sword;
but the tongue of the wise brings healing.*

PROVERBS 27:17
Iron sharpens iron, and one man sharpens another.

Based on the five passages you just read, what is the result of using our words to encourage our spouses?

With these verses in mind, write down a list of good character traits you believe your spouse has on one side of separate pieces of paper. On the other side list some of your biggest concerns or fears you and your spouse have about yourselves.

For example, the husband will write good character traits he believes his wife has on one side of the paper and on the other side he'll write down his biggest concerns or fears he has about himself. Once both spouses have completed the activity, share and discuss with each other. Use this exercise as an opportunity to put into practice what you read in the verses about encouragement.

> Use the space below and document this experience. Pray for each other and encourage your spouse in his or her best character traits. Help build each other up where you may feel like you fall short.

Date Night

Date nights are important and should be a staple in your marriage. They are also fun and a great way to deepen your connection with your spouse. Choose one (or both) of the following date night ideas to do before the next group session.

OPTION 1—TANDEM BIKE RIDING

Find a local bike rental place that will allow you to rent a tandem bike for at least 30 minutes. Tandem bike riding is great exercise, not just physically. It's also a great way to discover more about each other in marriage.

CONVERSATION STARTER: How can we better understand each other and see things from the other's perspective?

OPTION 2—LOVE LANGUAGES DINNER DATE OR DATES

Discovering the things that make each of you feel loved is a major part of knowing your spouse better. Dr. Gary Chapman has a great book, *The Five Love Languages: How to Express Heartfelt Commitment to Your Mate* (Northfield Press, 2004), that teaches couples how to discover each person's love language. He's also created an assessment for busy couples to learn their love languages. Complete the assessment over dinner and discuss or have a series of at-home reading dates where you read through a chapter of the book each night and discuss.

CONVERSATION STARTER: When do you feel most loved? How can I show my love for you?

SESSION 5:
PERSEVERING

"... for better or for worse, for richer or for poorer, in sickness and in health ..."

Those are probably the most unforgettable words said in a couple's wedding vows. Yet, it seems we do forget. We forget we made that promise. We forget that challenges are inevitable.

It should be understood, based on our wedding vows and the percentage of married couples that divorce, that we'll experience challenges in our marriages. That's why we vow to our spouses that we will be there and will still love them *when*—not *if*—these challenges arise. You probably agree that it's much easier said than done.

A lasting and truly fulfilling marriage is only formed through PerseveRING.

START

Welcome to the fifth group session. Session 4 focused on knowing our spouses better through effective communication and intentionally studying them.

> What was most helpful, encouraging, or challenging from your couple time activities from the previous session?

In this session we'll begin to focus on the challenges we face in marriage and how we can not just make it through them, but grow closer together through these experiences.

WATCH

GOAL: **To grow through your challenges in marriage, equipping you to use these challenges to make your marriage better.**

WATCH SESSION 5: "PERSEVERING." **Use the statements below to follow along and record key quotes and ideas that stand out to you on the notes page.**

> We must understand that marriage is hard and takes work, but great rewards come as a result.

> The way you handle conflict can determine the success or failure of your marriage.

> Once you are broken in marriage, you are primed to be used by God in a new way.

> Joyfully remembering the promises you made will help when facing challenges.

> There will be storms, so prepare yourself.

> Knowing how to deal with unmet expectations can lead to more fulfillment in your marriage.

DISCUSS

Trials or struggles are hardly viewed as positive experiences, yet the Bible paints a beautiful picture of them.

In fact struggles, trials, and hard work are part of the development process God uses to get the most out of us and the best for us. These difficulties are necessary in God's way of doing things. This includes our marriages as well. As we experience and embrace this we can approach challenges in our marriages from a completely different viewpoint.

Let's take a look at some of the passages that illustrate this and discuss how they apply to each of our marriages.

READ JAMES 1:2 AND 1 PETER 4:12.

Every common English version of the Bible translates James 1:2 using a form of the word "when." The word "if" is not used. Peter also tells us not to be surprised when we are tested.

Based on these word choices, what can you be assured of regarding trials?

READ JAMES 1:2-4 AND ROMANS 5:3-5.

What should our attitudes be when we experience trials in our marriages?

What is produced from our trials?

Think of a time when you faced a trial with a positive attitude, and a time when you didn't. How does one's attitude make a difference?

READ JAMES 1:5 AND PROVERBS 3:5-6.

If you are unsure of what to do, or how to handle a trial in your marriage, what is a good plan of action according to these verses?

WRAP-UP

We can expect to face trials in our marriages.

Our challenging experiences are what God uses
to mature us individually and as a couple.

We can and should choose joy even in the midst of trials
because something amazing will be produced.

PRAY

Spend the next few minutes praying with and for one another. Use the points below for guidance.

Thank God for how He is working in your marriage through your trials.

Ask God to help you see your trials the way He sees them.

Pray for couples in your group and around the world to hold on, to not give up, and to let God complete His work in them.

Thank God for His grace, which has allowed you to persevere during the tough times of your marriage.

MARRIAGE ENRICHMENT ACTIVITIES

ACTIVITY 1

READ GALATIANS 6:9.

*So we must not get tired of doing good, for we will
reap at the proper time if we don't give up.*

On the left side of the chart below, make a list of times when you
wanted to quit something, but you didn't. Do this individually first and
then as a couple. Your list can include experiences that happened prior
to or during marriage.

On the right side of the chart, list all the good things that happened as a
result of those experiences and not giving up.

TRIALS	RESULTS

Why do we think we will be immune to trials?

What are the benefits of continuing to do good in times of trial and in times of ease?

What is the greatest lesson you learned through a time of trial?

Close this activity by encouraging each other as a couple and praying that you will have perseverance through the hard times of marriage.

_____

_____

_____

_____

_____

_____

_____

_____

READ PHILIPPIANS 4:12-13.

I know both how to have a little, and I know how to have a lot. In any and all circumstances I have learned the secret of being content—whether well fed or hungry, whether in abundance or in need. I am able to do all things through Him who strengthens me.

What is the most challenging thing you've faced as individuals? As a married couple? What is the most challenging thing you've faced in your marriage?

Discuss what happened as a result of those challenges. If you were able to overcome this challenge, how did you do this?

If you were not able to overcome it, what prevented you from doing so?

Share your thoughts on how you can better handle the next challenge in your marriage. What are specific ways to find contentment in the midst of challenges?

Jesus is the One who strengthens us and gives us what we need to persevere. He is the One to guide us through any and all challenges and circumstances. Thank Him for being all we need for contentment and purpose in life.

_____
_____
_____
_____
_____
_____
_____
_____
_____
_____
_____
_____
_____
_____
_____
_____

READ GENESIS 50:20.

You planned evil against me; God planned it for good to bring about the present result—the survival of many people.

Now skim through the story of Joseph in Genesis to discover how he came to this point in his life. Notice in the chart below all of the different trials Joseph had to face.

SCRIPTURE	SITUATION
GENESIS 37:1-4	HATED BY BROTHERS
GENESIS 37:26-37	SOLD INTO SLAVERY
GENESIS 39:1-12	FACED TEMPTATION
GENESIS 39:13-20	WRONGLY ACCUSED
GENESIS 41:41-56	STRUGGLE TO THE TOP
GENESIS 45:1-15	RESTORATION WITH FAMILY
GENESIS 50:20	SAVES MANY LIVES

READ GENESIS 39:2, 21.

What do you discover about Joseph from these two verses?

Sometimes the culture, other people, or even well-meaning friends and family members introduce trials and challenges into our marriage, but even through these struggles, we need to remember that God has a plan and He is with us.

Pray and ask God to show you what He wants you to know about the trials you face. Ask Him to help you both be more like Joseph in regard to challenges in your marriage.

After you pray, use the space below to write down some practical steps you can take the next time you are faced with a challenge in your marriage.

Date Night

Date nights are important and should be a staple in your marriage. They are also fun and a great way to deepen your connection with your spouse. Choose one (or both) of the following date night ideas to do before the next group session.

OPTION 1—SWEAT IT OUT

This date is intended to push you to your limits, like we are often pushed in marriage. Go for a run, take a fitness class, hit the gym, take a kickboxing class, or try something else that physically challenges you and causes you to push through and persevere.

CONVERSATION STARTER: Read Hebrews 12:1-2 and discuss how it relates to your marriage.

OPTION 2—WATCH A SPORTING EVENT, LIVE PERFORMANCE, OR DOCUMENTARY

If you are unable to do the physical activities suggested in the first date night option, then another option is to watch those who do. The most successful athletes and performers push their bodies and their minds to their limits.

Successful people in all walks of life go through major challenges along the way. For this date, observe these people perform in person or on television. You could also read about them and discuss how their training and their struggles helped them mature and reach new levels.

CONVERSATION STARTER: Read 1 Corinthians 9:24-27 and discuss how it relates to your marriage.

SESSION 6:
RESTORING

"Be prepared to continue to give, be able to forgive, and to experience more and more joy."

You probably know this by now, but when you commit your life to someone in marriage you should be prepared to forgive. "All have sinned and fall short of the glory of God" (Rom. 3:23) includes you and your spouse. There is so much promise and so much bliss during the engagement, your wedding day, and your honeymoon seasons that the need for forgiveness might seem impossible.

If only it were possible to maintain that level of optimism and hope. But we are human. Whether intended or not, married people hurt each other. Hearts are broken. Trust is tested. Thankfully, restoration is available to us, and this restoration can be the catalyst for coming together as one like you've never done before.

RestoRING the broken pieces happens in the process of growing a long-lasting and fulfilling marriage.

START

Welcome to the sixth group session. Session 5 focused on understanding that trials will come in our marriages, how we should view them, and how God will use them to mature us and our marriages.

> What was most helpful, encouraging, or challenging from your couple time activities from the previous session?

Those trials we talked about in Session 5 can break us, especially when they come from our spouse. In this session we'll begin to focus on restoring the broken areas in our marriage.

WATCH

GOAL: To learn why and how we should work to restore broken areas in our marriage quickly through repentance and forgiveness.

WATCH SESSION 6: "RESTORING." Use the statements below to follow along and record key quotes and ideas that stand out to you on the notes page.

> Realize you both make mistakes and have hurt each other at some point.

> Standing on your foundation is the key to restoration.

> Prayer and confession are powerful tools for restoration in your marriage.

> Holding on to anger opens the door to negativity in your marriage.

> Restoration takes action on both the offending and the offended spouse.

DISCUSS

We've all had people do or say things to us we didn't appreciate, or that even hurt us. The less intimate that relationship is the easier the situation is to handle, but when the hurt comes from someone close to you, it gets tougher. However, it doesn't get any tougher than when it is your spouse.

Nobody can make us feel as good as our spouses do—and no one can hurt us as bad. We all need grace and to intentionally work at restoring our relationship when we've been hurt, disappointed, or wronged.

Let's take a look at some of the passages that illustrate mutual need for grace and restoration and discuss how they apply to each of our marriages.

READ ROMANS 3:23 AND MATTHEW 7:1-5.

What do these passages teach you about judging others and their mistakes?

What should the proper response be when your spouse does something wrong or hurtful if you respond according to these verses?

READ JAMES 5:9-20.

Based on verses 13-15, what is one key to restoring a person who has done wrong?

If it is you who has caused the hurt or pain, what should you do according to verse 16?

What happens when you handle your own offenses, and your spouse's, in this manner?

READ MATTHEW 18:21-22.

At what point does this verse tell you that it's OK to stop forgiving?

What do you think happens in your marriage if you stop forgiving when your spouse wrongs you?

What are practical ways you can be more intentional in your marriage to pray, confess, and forgive?

WRAP-UP

There will be times when our spouses hurt us and when we hurt them.

At no point should our love or actions to our spouses be dictated by their wrongdoings.

Prayer and confession are keys to true restoration in our marriages.

PRAY

Spend the next few minutes praying with and for one another. Use the points below for guidance.

Thank God for His grace in your life and in your marriage.

Ask God for the strength to impart the same grace He's given you to your spouse.

Ask God to heal anyone who is caught in a perpetual sin in his or her marriage.

Pray that God will restore broken areas in your marriage, as well as the marriages in your group and around the world.

MARRIAGE ENRICHMENT ACTIVITIES

ACTIVITY 1

READ NEHEMIAH 1; 2:1-5.

Based on Nehemiah's prayer in chapter 1, why were the people in Jerusalem living in such poor conditions?

What did God promise He would do if the people returned to Him?

READ NEHEMIAH 2:16-18.

How do the priests, nobles, and officials respond to Nehemiah's charge to rebuild the wall?

Both Nehemiah and Jerusalem's leaders desired the restoration of the city and were encouraged to rebuild the walls together. Let's see how this principle can be applied to your marriage. With your spouse, find something around your house that needs to be rebuilt or repaired. Discuss what you will need to start and finish the repair. Begin working on this project together before the next session. It is OK if this project is not something you can finish before the next session. Keep working together until you have completed it.

Use the space below and document your experience working together.

Compare and contrast your project with your marriage. Why is this repair and restoring easier with two people? How does working together strengthen your marriage?

_____

_____

_____

_____

_____

_____

_____

_____

_____

_____

_____

_____

_____

READ ROMANS 15:4-6 BELOW AND UNDERLINE THE WORDS IN THE PASSAGE THAT YOU WOULD WANT TO USE TO DESCRIBE YOUR MARRIAGE.

For whatever was written in the past was written for our instruction, so that we may have hope through endurance and through the encouragement from the Scriptures. Now may the God who gives endurance and encouragement allow you to live in harmony with one another, according to the command of Christ Jesus, so that you may glorify the God and Father of our Lord Jesus Christ with a united mind and voice.

If you have young kids who play with Legos® find one of their sets (without any pieces missing). If you don't have kids or complete Lego® sets, find the nearest toy store and buy a small set. Use the included step-by-step instructions to build the suggested design. Then take it all apart, mix them up, and get rid of the instructions. Then try to rebuild the design.

Did you endure through the project until the work was completed? Why or why not?

Once rebuilt, if you are able to do so, discuss the challenges you had while rebuilding the design without the instructions.

What truth in Romans 15:4-6 can be applied to marriage?

What happens to our marriage when we try to live without consulting the instructions of God's Word and obeying them?

Use the space below and document any other truth you learned from the Lego® building. Then spend time praying for "harmony with one another" and a "united mind and voice" in your marriage and in Christ.

_____

_____

_____

_____

_____

_____

_____

_____

_____

_____

_____

_____

_____

ACTIVITY 3

READ NEHEMIAH 6:15-16.

The wall was completed in 52 days, on the twenty-fifth day of the month Elul. When all our enemies heard this, all the surrounding nations were intimidated and lost their confidence, for they realized that this task had been accomplished by our God.

Who was ultimately responsible for rebuilding the wall in Jerusalem?

Who is ultimately responsible for rebuilding and restoring what is broken in your marriage?

Refer back to your notes from the group time in Session 2 about building our marriages on the Rock and your marriage's foundational verse. Read your verse(s) and pray together, asking God to help you keep Him at the center of your marriage. Write out your prayers in the space below.

Ask God to show you what you need to do to restore any broken areas in your marriage. Discuss them in love and write down what you believe God has revealed to you both through what you've read, prayed, and shared.

Pray and thank God that He is a God who restores what is broken.

_____
_____
_____
_____
_____
_____
_____
_____
_____
_____
_____
_____
_____
_____
_____
_____
_____
_____

Date Night

Date nights are important and should be a staple in your marriage. They are also fun and a great way to deepen your connection with your spouse. Choose one (or both) of the following date night ideas to do before the next group session.

OPTION 1—MOVIE NIGHT

Read and discuss Ephesians 5:22-33. After reading and discussing together, enjoy a *Fireproof* movie night. This movie is a great story of restoration in marriage. After watching the movie discuss how the husband and wife lived out the passage in Ephesians 5.

CONVERSATION STARTER: **How can we make our marriage affair-proof?**

OPTION 2—VOLUNTEER YOUR TIME FOR A HOME BUILDING OR RESTORING PROJECT

Reread Nehemiah 1; 2:1-5. Nehemiah was deeply affected when he learned what his people were going through and the living conditions they were enduring because of their broken situation. He understood their plight was caused by their sin and turning from God. Yet God promised if they returned to Him, He would restore them. God answered their prayers, and Nehemiah sacrificed his time to help rebuild the wall.

For this date night option, pray for an opportunity to help someone build or restore something. Choose a day to volunteer your time and resources to help. Discuss the experience together.

CONVERSATION STARTER: **What is one thing we can do today that will make us better tomorrow?**

SESSION 7:
PROSPE*RING*

"May this couple ... experience more joy with each
passing day, with each passing year."

Our hope on our wedding day and throughout our marriage is for our joy to continue to
grow. It's the happily ever after that is depicted in movies. It's the dream marriage. Joy—
every day and every year.

The great news is that overwhelming joy is not only possible in movies. It's possible
for you and everyone who commits to a life together in marriage. The "catch" is it may
not look like what we thought it would look like. We'll still face challenges, but it's still
amazing, fulfilling, and the stuff dreams are made of.

After all you've experienced in marriage you are now prospeRING in your relationship.
What a phenomenal ring this is.

Welcome to the seventh group session. Session 6 focused on restoring the broken areas in our marriages through repentance and forgiveness.

> What was most helpful, encouraging, or challenging from your couple time activities from the previous session?

In this session we'll begin to focus on the amazing blessing of marriage.

WATCH

GOAL: To view our marriages in all their glory and appreciate our spouses and how God has blessed us with this wonderful thing called marriage.

WATCH SESSION 7: "PROSPERING." Use the statements below to follow along and record key quotes and ideas that stand out to you on the notes page.

> We have the opportunity to choose joy in all circumstances in our marriages.

> Remaining in love requires our action, regardless of our feelings.

> Our love can continue to grow with each experience and each challenge.

> Reflecting on your marriage will give you a greater appreciation for the hard times.

> Prospering in marriage happens over time.

DISCUSS

We've discussed the reality that marriage is hard. We've experienced hurts and challenges from all angles. And we've probably all witnessed a couple separate or divorce because their marriage didn't meet their expectations and they made a choice to end it.

But marriage can be amazing! There isn't a relationship on this earth that compares. Two people coming together as one is something only God could have created. Marriage is blessed by God, marriage is fulfilling, and at its best, marriage is full of love.

READ 1 CORINTHIANS 13:4-8.

In 1 Corinthians, we are given a picture of love in action. Love is not depicted as a reactive feeling but as several willful actions.

Based on this passage, in what ways do you love your spouse well?

In what ways could you love him or her better?

READ PROVERBS 18:22 AND 2 CORINTHIANS 13:11 AND THEN DISCUSS THE FOLLOWING QUESTIONS.

While you and your spouse are both sinners, the institution of marriage as God created it is inherently good and comes with favor from the Lord.

Do you view your marriage in this way? Why or why not?

How do Paul's closing words to the Corinthians apply to our marriages?

What would you consider a mature marriage to be?

Where should our joy come from and our hope for a mature marriage?

Marriage is a blessing from God.

We should rejoice in our marriages and the relationship God has given us with our spouses.

In everything we experience, good and bad, our joy can remain and our hope can increase in Christ.

PRAY

Spend the next few minutes praying with and for one another. Use the points below for guidance.

Praise God for the institution of marriage and for protecting it in the lives of those who choose to put Him at the center.

Ask for forgiveness for anytime you've viewed your marriage as something other than good.

Ask God to increase the joy and hope in your marriage.

Ask God to allow couples in your group and around the world to experience the joy and hope that is found in marriage.

Pray that your perspective on your marriage will always be viewed through the lens of God's grace.

MARRIAGE ENRICHMENT ACTIVITIES

ACTIVITY 1

This activity is for married couples. Engaged and unmarried couples, please skip to Activity 2.

READ GENESIS 2:24; PROVERBS 5:18; AND 1 CORINTHIANS 7:5.

GENESIS 2:24
This is why a man leaves his father and mother and bonds with his wife, and they become one flesh.

PROVERBS 5:18
Let your fountain be blessed, and take pleasure in the wife of your youth.

1 CORINTHIANS 7:5A
Do not deprive one another sexually—except when you agree for a time, to devote yourselves to prayer.

Is sex a blessing or a burden in your marriage? Explain your answer.

We've been given a unique way to show the oneness God has called us to in marriage through sexual intercourse. This week's first activity is our opportunity to do this. But this activity is not just for today. I'm challenging you as a couple to rejoice in this "gift" every day this week. What better way to love your spouse and enjoy your marriage this week. No need to report on this when you meet again for the final session!

REREAD 1 THESSALONIANS 5:16-18 AND PHILIPPIANS 4:4 FROM YOUR GROUP TIME.

1 THESSALONIANS 5:16-18
Rejoice always! Pray constantly. Give thanks in everything, for this is God's will for you in Christ Jesus.

PHILIPPIANS 4:4
Rejoice in the Lord always. I will say it again: Rejoice!

How do you describe always rejoicing and rejoicing in all things in your marriage?

On a scale from 1-6 (6 being the most intentional), how are you doing so far this week in this area of your marriage? How are you intentional about looking for joy and ways to rejoice?

1	2	3	4	5	6

What are some areas where you are lacking joy? How can you seek joy and contentment even when your marriage or life is not continuously joyful?

READ EPHESIANS 1:15-19.

In this prayer for spiritual insight, Paul lets the Ephesian church know he is praying for them and that he is thankful for them.

READ VERSE 16.

> *I never stop giving thanks for you as I remember you in my prayers.*

How are you expressing joy and thankfulness to your spouse? How might you pray for your spouse's spiritual growth?

To put this principle into action, express your joy and thankfulness for your spouse this week via text messages or short handwritten note. Every day until the next session send your spouse a text or note with a reason you are thankful for them and how they give you joy.

Spend time praying together this week that God will multiply the joy in your marriage and that you will grow in gratitude for one another.

READ JOHN 15:13 AND EPHESIANS 5:25-33.

JOHN 15:13

No one has greater love than this, that someone would lay down his life for his friends.

EPHESIANS 5:25-33

Husbands, love your wives, just as Christ loved the church and gave Himself for her to make her holy, cleansing her with the washing of water by the word. He did this to present the church to Himself in splendor, without spot or wrinkle or anything like that, but holy and blameless. In the same way, husbands are to love their wives as their own bodies. He who loves his wife loves himself. For no one ever hates his own flesh but provides and cares for it, just as Christ does for the church, since we are members of His body.

For this reason a man will leave his father and mother and be joined to his wife, and the two will become one flesh. This mystery is profound, but I am talking about Christ and the church. To sum up, each one of you is to love his wife as himself, and the wife is to respect her husband.

We've been given a true model for a prospering marriage—Christ and the church. Our marriages are to look like the relationship between Christ and the church.

Wives: How should you relate to your husbands based on this passage?
Husbands: How should you relate to your wives based on this passage?

Based on these two passages, what is the greatest love?

If you're reading this, then it's safe to assume you haven't been required to physically lay your life down for your spouse, but when in your marriage have you shown this type of sacrificial love? What impact did it have on your marriage?

We are called to serve our spouses sacrificially and to love them as we love ourselves. At times this may require a major sacrifice on our part. Most days we can do this by intentionally serving them with love.

To demonstrate this practically, for this activity you are going to serve your spouse by doing one of his or her primary tasks or household chores. So, if your wife vacuums the floors each week, then fellas take over the job and give her a break. Wives, if your husband usually takes out the garbage, take out the garbage for him.

Use the space below and document this experience serving each other, and then spend time in prayer this week asking God to help you love your spouse as Christ loves you.

Date Night

Date nights are important and should be a staple in your marriage. They are also fun and a great way to deepen your connection with your spouse. Choose one (or both) of the following date night ideas to do before the next group session.

OPTION 1—"TREAT YOURSELF" DATE NIGHT

Hebrews 13:4 says marriage should be honored. During the group sessions we discussed how our marriages are reasons for joy. For this date night, go to your favorite place and treat yourselves to your favorite things (go to a favorite restaurant, take a walk in the park, etc.). Celebrate your marriage and each other in a great way.

CONVERSATION STARTER: If we could go anywhere in the world and live for one month, where would you want to go?

OPTION 2—HORSE AND CARRIAGE RIDE OR DRIVE

Search for a local business that offers horse and carriage rides. Put on some of your best clothes and make a big deal about it. Go grab a bite to eat and then cap it off with a romantic ride in the horse and carriage. While riding, take some selfies and discuss all the reasons you have to be happy about your marriage. For areas where this option isn't available, take a long drive together before or after you eat. Spend time enjoying the scenery and each other.

CONVERSATION STARTER: How has marriage been a blessing?

SESSION 8:
MENTO*RING*

"We hope they have the loving assistance of their family, the constant support of friends ..."

Much like it takes a village to raise a child, it takes the friendship, support, and accountability of others to have a successful marriage. Those who have worn the first six rings wouldn't have been able to do so without other couples or trusted family and friends to help them along the way.

Your marriage is bigger than you, so no matter which ring you're wearing, you have an opportunity—an obligation—to help someone else.

The MentoRING is where you connect with others and show them what a lasting and fulfilling marriage looks like and how to make it happen.

START

Welcome to the eighth group session. Session 7 focused on the joy we can have in marriage through a relationship with God and our spouse.

> What was most helpful, encouraging, or challenging from your couple time activities from the previous session?

In this session we'll begin to focus on using our marriage experiences to be an example and a blessing to others. Be willing to allow God to use your marriage.

WATCH

GOAL: To allow God to use our marriages to help other couples and to reveal His glory through how we relate to our spouses.

WATCH SESSION 8: "MENTORING." Use the statements below to follow along and record key quotes and ideas that stand out to you on the notes page.

> You do have something to share that can benefit other couples.

> Realizing your marriage is bigger than you and acting on that will add another level of fulfillment to your marriage.

> Consistently connecting with other couples on multiple levels is important: mentees, peers, and mentors.

> God will use your marriage to play a significant part in the advancement of His kingdom.

> Our marriages are not meant to function in isolation.

DISCUSS

Living a life that is a blessing to others is a full life. Living a marriage that is a blessing to other marriages is a full marriage. This is part of our call as married couples. We are to receive, relate, and reciprocate with other couples. Perhaps another couple has helped you, or walked side-by-side with you, through a difficult season. Now it's your turn to do the same.

Let's take a look at some of the passages that illustrate this and discuss how they apply to each of our marriages.

READ PHILIPPIANS 4:9 AND 2 TIMOTHY 2:2.

We don't have to be marriage counselors or have the perfect marriage to be an example and a blessing to other couples.

> What did Paul say the Philippians were to do with what they had learned from him? What did Paul instruct Timothy to do with what he had heard?
>
> Who do you know that is a role model, an example who does this well in relation to marriage? What are some practical ways you can be an example to others in your marriages?

READ ECCLESIASTES 4:7-12.

In the "Facebook age" we are bombarded with what seems to be perfect images of our peers. Ecclesiastes 4:7-8 touches on the trap of "keeping up with the Joneses." Instead of competing or trying to impress, we should come alongside other couples. Verses 9-12 illustrate the benefits of this.

> How are couples hurt when we compare and compete with one another? What are some benefits of experiencing life with other couples and helping and lifting up one another?

READ TITUS 2:2-8 AND PSALM 145:4.

> Who has helped you or been a mentor in your marriage? Take time to share with the group lessons you have learned from other couples— older couples, counselors, friends, or even another couple in this group.

READ 1 THESSALONIANS 2:8 AND PROVERBS 11:25.

Whether or not you think you have it "figured out," you have a responsibility to other couples. For us to experience ups, downs, challenges, accomplishments, sadness, discovering, commitment, betrayal, love, and God's grace in our marriages and not help others prepare for and experience the same is almost a crime.

What are some lessons you've learned in marriage that could be beneficial to another couple?

What happens when you pour into others?

WRAP-UP

Your marriage is blessed to be a blessing.

Seeking to build peer-to-peer, mentee, and mentor relationships adds fulfillment to your marriage.

Your marriage plays a significant role in God's kingdom and perfect plan.

PRAY

Spend the next few minutes praying with and for one another. Use the points below for guidance.

Praise God for allowing you to connect with this group and for what He's revealed to you through the *7 Rings of Marriage*.

Pray for God to open your eyes and hearts to another couple or couples with whom you can share your story.

Ask God to give you boldness when sharing what He's done in your marriage.

Thank God for your marriage, for making it last, and for allowing you and your spouse to experience Him at a new level.

MARRIAGE ENRICHMENT ACTIVITIES

ACTIVITY 1

READ MATTHEW 28:16-20.

> *The 11 disciples traveled to Galilee, to the mountain where*
> *Jesus had directed them. When they saw Him, they worshiped,*
> *but some doubted. Then Jesus came near and said to them,*
> *"All authority has been given to Me in heaven and on earth. Go,*
> *therefore, and make disciples of all nations, baptizing them in*
> *the name of the Father and of the Son and of the Holy Spirit,*
> *teaching them to observe everything I have commanded you.*
> *And remember, I am with you always, to the end of the age."*

Throughout the Bible we see examples of people sharing their knowledge and experiences with others, praying for one another, and holding one another accountable. God commands us to teach to others what we have learned from Him.

God has given you power to minister to other couples. This mentoring may be in the form of you modeling and teaching your children what a God-honoring marriage looks like. It may be mentoring close friends or the couple next door. God may even open the door for you to teach, speak, write, or run a full-fledged marriage ministry.

God has given you a unique ministry in your marriage to reach certain couples. Your one activity after this group session is to pray and ask God to reveal several couples for you to share what you've learned through this Bible study. Write their names down, begin praying for them, and connect with them on a couple-to-couple basis, or in a small group like this. If you feel God is leading you to take those couples through this study then speak with your group leader to help you get started.

Use the space below to write the names of these couples.

Commit to pray for them on a regular basis and pray for wisdom in your ministry to them.

Date Night

I hope you've taken advantage of the date night options provided throughout this study. Date nights are important and must remain a staple in your marriage no matter what stage or ring you are wearing.

For this last session, I'm only giving you one option for date night. Enjoy!

GROUP CELEBRATION DATE

Have a group date with some or all of the couples who went through this study with you. Choose one of the previous dates or do something completely new. Enjoy each other's company and celebrate each other's marriages together.

LEADER TIPS

Whether you are just starting a Bible study or continuing to grow groups in your church, we are so grateful for your investment in enrichment of marriages. Thanks for choosing LifeWay studies, and specifically, *The 7 Rings of Marriage* by Jackie Bledsoe. This study can be used in a variety of settings, including your church, home, office, or favorite coffee shop. So where do you begin?

PRAY, PRAY, PRAY. As you prepare to lead this Bible study, know that prayer is essential. Spend time asking God to work in the hearts and lives of couples who will participate in the study. Immediately begin to learn what issues these couples are facing and pray about what will help them grow spiritually. Continue to pray throughout the study and encourage the couples to include prayer as a daily spiritual discipline. Ask God to lead you to the couples that He has called.

TALK TO YOUR PASTOR OR CHURCH LEADER. Ask for their input, prayers, and support.

SECURE YOUR LOCATION. Think about the number of people you can accommodate in the designated location. Reserve any tables, chairs, or needed media equipment for watching the videos from Jackie at *www.lifeway.com/7Rings*.

PROVIDE CHILDCARE. If you are inviting couples who have young children, this is essential!

PROVIDE RESOURCES. Order the needed number of Bible study books. You might get a few extra for last minute drop-ins.

PLAN AND PREPARE. Become familiar with the Bible study. Preview the videos at *www.lifeway.com/7Rings* or in the DVD leader kit. Prepare the outline you will follow based on the leader materials available. Go to *www.lifeway.com/7Rings* to find free extra leader resources.

BE CONSIDERATE OF REMARRIED COUPLES. A marriage study can be challenging for couples who've experienced divorce. Some topics of divorce and the biblical view can become uncomfortable. Reassure them that there is no judgment or condemnation and remind them that in spite of their past the marriage they are in now is the marriage the principles discussed are referring to.

LEAD. One of the best things you can do as the leader is set the pace for this study. Be consistent and trustworthy. Encourage the couples to follow through on the study, to attend the group sessions, and hold one another accountable to do their activities between sessions. Accept couples where they are but also set expectations that motivate commitment. Listen carefully and be responsible with the discussions and sharing within the group. Keep confidences shared within the group. Be honest and vulnerable with the group and share what God is teaching you. Most couples will follow your lead and be more willing to share and participate when they see your example.

FOLLOW UP BETWEEN SESSIONS. Throughout the study, stay engaged with the couples in your group. Use social media, emails, or even a quick note in the mail to connect with one another and share prayer needs. Let them know when you are praying specifically for them.

CELEBRATE AND SHARE. As a group, share what God is teaching you. Use #7RingsStudy on social media to connect with other couples doing the study.

EVALUATE. What went well? What could be improved upon? How did the couples in your group respond?

NEXT STEPS. Even after the study concludes, follow up with the couples in your group. You may even provide additional opportunities for them to connect with other Bible studies.

Go to *jackiebledsoe.com/7RingsResources* for a free marriage devotional and more marriage resources.

KEY INSIGHTS

SESSION ONE

- Your marriage has a God-given purpose.
- God created Eve to be Adam's perfect complement and helper. One of the primary roles in your marriage, whether husband or wife, is to serve your spouse.
- Your marriage can be fruitful and fulfilling, no matter the circumstances, but you have to know its purpose and keep your eyes set on what God can accomplish.

SESSION TWO

- Our marriages are best when they are set on the Rock—on our faith in Christ.
- The actions in our marriage must be carefully and consistently measured against the principles of the Bible—God's blueprint for our lives and marriages.

SESSION THREE

- Becoming one with your spouse is God's plan for marriage.
- We should not allow anything to come between us and our spouses.
- Getting help is not bad, it is actually one of the wisest things we can do.

SESSION FOUR

- We must know our spouses—who they are in Christ and who they are in relationship to us.
- Effective communication can be a bridge or a barrier to better knowing our spouses.
- The practice of studying our spouses and our marriage must be a priority.

SESSION FIVE

- We can expect to face trials in our marriages.
- Our challenging experiences are what God uses to mature us individually and as a couple.
- We can and should choose joy even in the midst of trials because something amazing will be produced.

SESSION SIX

- There will be times when our spouses hurt us and when we hurt them.
- At no point should our love or actions to our spouses be dictated by their wrongdoings.
- Prayer and confession are keys to true restoration in our marriages.

SESSION SEVEN

- Marriage is a blessing from God.
- We should rejoice in our marriages and the relationship God has given us with our spouses.
- In everything we experience, good and bad, our joy can remain and our hope can increase in Christ.

SESSION EIGHT

- Your marriage is blessed to be a blessing.
- Seeking to build peer-to-peer, mentee, and mentor relationships adds fulfillment to your marriage.
- Your marriage plays a significant role in God's kingdom and perfect plan.

ADDITIONAL CONVERSATION STARTERS

- What is your favorite movie and why?

- What is the most annoying habit someone can have?

- What is your favorite season and why?

- If you could be any animal, what would you be and why?

- If you had a theme song for your life or intro music that followed you around, what would it be?

- What smell brings back the greatest memories for you?

- Name one person that you would like to be stuck in an elevator with and what you would talk about.

- What is one of the funniest experiences you've ever had?

- What were your favorite cartoons as a child?

- If you could be on a TV show, what character would you like to play?

- What is your favorite song?

- What is the strangest thing you've ever eaten?

- What has helped society the most in the last 10 years?

- What has hurt society the most?

- What is your favorite sport to play or watch?

- What is a goal you have for the next 5 years?

- What is one of the craziest things you've accomplished so far in your life?

- If we could really time travel, what time period and place would you like to visit?

- What is the best thing to do on a cold, wintry day?

- What were some of your favorite family traditions growing up? What are some you would like to start?

- If time froze for everyone but you, how would you live that day?

- If one of us was hurt in a debilitating accident, what would we do?

- My favorite memory of our wedding day is ...

- The most challenging aspect of my spiritual life is ...

- What is one thing you would change about me?

- If you could have one superpower what would it be?

- The scariest moment of my life was …

- What is one smell you absolutely love?

- Which of the 7 Rings of Marriage do you think we are wearing right now?

FURTHER RESOURCES

HomeLife magazine*

ParentLife magazine**

Mature Living magazine

The Five Love Languages: How to Express Heartfelt Commitment to Your Mate by Dr. Gary Chapman

Love and Respect: The Love She Most Desires, the Respect He Desperately Needs by Emerson Eggerichs

What the Bible Says About Love, Marriage, and Sex by David Jeremiah

Experiencing God at Home by Richard Blackaby and Tom Blackaby

The Love Dare journal and *The Love Dare Bible Study* by Michael Catt, Stephen Kendrick, and Alex Kendrick

The Love Dare for Parents Bible Study by Stephen Kendrick and Alex Kendrick

The Resolution for Men by Randy Alcorn, Stephen Kendrick, and Alex Kendrick

The Resolution for Women by Priscilla Shirer

Intimacy: Understanding a Woman's Heart by Kenny Luck

Go to *jackiebledsoe.com/7RingsResources* for a free marriage devotional and more marriage resources.

For Married Women Only: Three Principles for Honoring Your Husband
  by Tony Evans

*Men Are Like Waffles, Women Are Like Spaghetti: Understanding and Delighting in Your
  Differences* by Bill and Pam Farrel

The Secret to the Marriage You Want: The Trading Places Small Group Experience by Les
  and Leslie Parrott

Extraordinary Marriage: God's Plan for Your Journey by Rodney and Selma Wilson

For Women Only: The Bible Study: What You Need to Know About the Inner Lives of Men
  by Shaunti Feldhahn

For Young Women Only by Shaunti Feldhahn and Lisa A. Rice

*For Men Only Discussion Guide: A Companion to the Bestseller About
  the Inner Lives of Women* by Jeff Feldhahn, Shaunti Feldhahn, and Brian Smith

The 7 Rings of Marriage: Your Model for a Lasting and Fulfilling Marriage by Jackie Bledsoe

* Jackie Bledsoe is a regular contributor to *HomeLife*, LifeWay's faith and family magazine. In his
monthly column, "Love That Lasts," Jackie offers encouragement for couples in whatever "ring"
or stage of marriage they are in. *HomeLife* is available through your church or can be ordered at
lifeway.com/HomeLife.

**Jackie also regularly contributes to *ParentLife*, LifeWay's parenting magazine. In his monthly
column, "Dad's Life," Jackie offers encouragement and inspiration for dads. *ParentLife* is available
through your church or can be ordered at *LifeWay.com/ParentLife.*

SCHEDULE
JACKIE BLEDSOE
FOR YOUR NEXT EVENT!

JackieBledsoe.com/7RingsEvents

Jackie is quickly becoming the thought leader in matters of family and fatherhood. He is already an influence in my life.
THOM S. RAINER, PRESIDENT & CEO, LIFEWAY CHRISTIAN RESOURCES

His expertise adds so much to life! He helps you to engage with life, learn how to do life better and connect in a great way!
BETHANY PALMER, CO-CEO, THE MONEY COUPLE

Jackie will prompt you to see your responsibility as a husband and/or father in a new light!
KEVIN B. BULLARD, PRESIDENT, MARRIAGE WORKS!,
WWW.MARRIAGEWORKS.US